ALLEN COUNTY PUBLIC LIBRARY
FORT WAYNE, INDIANA 46802

You may return this book to any agency or branch
of the Allen County Public Library

DEMCO

ENDANGERED!

CHEETAHS

Shona Grimbly

Series Consultant: James G. Doherty
General Curator, The Bronx Zoo, New York

BENCHMARK BOOKS

MARSHALL CAVENDISH
NEW YORK

Benchmark Books
Marshall Cavendish Corporation
99 White Plains Road
Tarrytown, New York 10591-9001

Library of Congress Cataloging-in-Publication Data

Grimbly, Shona.
    Cheetahs / Shona Grimbly.
      p. cm. — (Endangered!)
    Includes bibliographic references (p.   ) and index.
    Summary: Describes the physical characteristics, habits, and natural environment of cheetahs and what is being done to protect these animals from complete extinction.
    ISBN 0-7614-0319-1 (lib. bdg.)
    1. Cheetah—Juvenile literature. 2. Endangered species—Juvenile literature. [1. Cheetah. 2. Endangered species.] I. Title. II. Series.
QL737.C23G75 1999
599.75'9—dc21

98-18773
CIP
AC

Printed in Hong Kong

PICTURE CREDITS
The publishers would like to thank the Natural History Photographic Agency (NHPA) for supplying all the photographs used in this book except for the following: 8, 10 AKG London; 9, 11 Mary Evans Picture Library.

Series created by Brown Packaging

Front cover: Cheetah's face showing tear stripe.
Title page: Cheetahs grooming.
Back cover: Cheetah in grassland.

Contents

Introduction

Cheetahs are the fastest animals on land. They are famous for being able to run at speeds of up to 70 miles per hour (113km/h). They belong to the cat **family**, which also includes lions, tigers, leopards, and the domestic cats many of us keep as pets in our homes.

Cheetahs are an endangered **species**. They used to live over much of Africa, Palestine, the Near East, and the Middle East as far as northern India. Today, they only survive in a few small areas of Africa south of the Sahara desert. There are still a few in Iran and perhaps in Egypt.

There are many reasons why there are so few cheetahs left. They used to be hunted and killed for their attractive

Perched high on a termite mound, these cheetahs are able to keep a lookout for prey and for predators.

coats. Also, as farming has spread over the areas where cheetahs live, there is less land for them to hunt on and fewer animals for them to eat.

There is only one species of cheetah, and its Latin name is *Acinonyx jubatus*. However, several **subspecies** have been described from Africa and Asia. The cheetah's name comes from an Indian word that means "spotted one."

The cheetah has a slender, graceful body, with a small head and ears. It has long, thin, powerful legs and large nostrils, lungs, and heart, all of which make it able to run

The length and power of the cheetah's legs make it able to cover the ground in bounding strides.

Area where cheetahs can be found

very fast. The claws on its paws act like running spikes. They help the cheetah sprint after its prey.

Most of the cheetah's fur is a light golden color, covered with small black spots. There

6

is a distinctive line running down each side of the animal's face, starting at the inner corner of the eye and finishing at the outer corner of the mouth. The fur on a young cheetah's neck is slightly longer, which makes it look a bit like a mane. A cheetah's paws are narrower than those of other cats. The pawpads are very hard and have ridges on them. The ridges give the cheetah extra grip when it is running.

An adult male cheetah is about $6^1/_4$ to $7^1/_4$ feet (1.9 to 2.2 m) long and weighs 86 to 130 pounds (39 to 59 kg). Its tail is about $2^1/_2$ feet (75 cm) long and is marked with black rings at the end. The females are slightly smaller.

Cheetahs are somewhat **adaptable**. They survive in semi-desert regions, grassland plains, or bushland. When they are not hunting, cheetahs are gentle and timid animals. They have never been known to attack humans.

Most cheetahs live on grassland plains, where their golden coats allow them to blend in with the background.

Cheetahs in History

In ancient times, cheetahs were common in India. There is evidence that people in India, Ancient Assyria, and Egypt all used cheetahs for hunting. Cheetahs were tamed and used as hunting animals from very early times in other places too. We know this because a very old silver vase decorated with a picture of a cheetah wearing a collar was found in an ancient burial mound in Central Asia. The vase was more than 2,000 years old. We also know that there were hunting cheetahs in Italy in the fifth century C.E.

Cheetahs are excellent hunters but are usually shy animals. The earliest human hunters probably followed cheetahs around and robbed them of their kills. Then the

This ancient Greek vase shows hunters with a tamed cheetah.

hunters decided to catch and tame the cheetahs to use them as hunting animals.

Cheetahs continued to be used as hunting animals right through the Middle Ages into the early Renaissance period. Akbar the Great, a Moghul emperor who ruled over India in the late 16th century, kept 3,000 cheetahs, which were trained to hunt antelope. In Europe, the great Emperor Charlemagne also used cheetahs for hunting.

When cheetahs were trained to become hunting animals, they were captured from the wild. This was easier than

In India, cheetahs were once used to hunt antelope for sport. They were trained to catch only male prey.

trying to breed them in captivity, which has always been difficult. The Moghul Emperor Jehangir Khan said that his father, Akbar the Great, could only get one pair out of his 3,000 cheetahs to **mate**, and they produced just three cheetah cubs.

The same method of catching and training cheetahs was used for hundreds of years. A rider on horseback would chase a wild cheetah until it became exhausted. Although cheetahs can run very fast in short bursts, they get tired quickly. When the cheetah was caught, a hood was slipped over its head and eyes so that it could not see. This made

In this 13th-century painting, the Mongol ruler Kublai Khan is shown hunting deer with a falcon and a cheetah.

the cheetah helpless. The captured cheetah would then be kept in a darkened room, where it relied on humans for its food and water. When the cheetah was fully tamed, it would be taken out and trained to hunt.

A hunting cheetah was always taken outside with a hood on. The hunters waited until the **prey** was in sight before taking the hood off. Then the cheetah would be released to catch the prey. If the cheetah was successful, it was given part of the kill as a reward. Some cheetahs may have tried to escape by running away. However, they soon tired and could easily be recaptured by a rider on horseback.

Trained cheetahs were kept tied up with their eyes covered until it was time for them to be released to catch the prey.

How Cheetahs Hunt

Cheetahs are **carnivores** and feed on small **ungulates**, such as impalas and gazelles, the young of larger ungulates, ground-living birds, and small **mammals** such as rodents. A female cheetah with young cubs to feed needs to hunt and kill every day if she can. Male cheetahs and females with no cubs eat on average every two to five days.

The cheetah usually hunts in the early morning or just before dusk to avoid the heat of the day. In short bursts, a cheetah can run at 50 to 70 miles per hour (80 to 113 km/h), but it can only keep up speeds this fast for a few hundred yards or meters. When it wants to make a kill, a cheetah chooses an animal and sprints from between 66 and 656 yards (60 and 600 m) away. Cheetahs need to see their prey

With its huge stride and ability to run in high-speed bursts, this cheetah can overtake a young antelope.

clearly because they hunt by sight rather than by smell or hearing. They avoid long grass and hunt on open areas where the grass is short.

The cheetah may walk towards its prey in full view, or it may **stalk** it unseen. Sometimes it will stay very still until the prey comes within **range**. When the prey is close enough, the cheetah launches its attack. With its long and strong legs, it has a loping stride that enables it to cover large distances quickly. With luck, the cheetah will overtake its prey and bring it to the ground by swiping at it with its powerful paws. Then the cheetah seizes the animal by its neck and chokes it by squeezing its windpipe.

This cheetah is pulling a freshly killed impala into cover to eat it undisturbed.

It is important that the cheetah's intended prey runs because it is then easier to select a possibly slower moving animal. Animals in tightly packed herds, such as zebras, are often not hunted by the cheetah. This could be because the cheetah has to choose one particular animal to attack, and this is difficult when a lot of animals are bunched together.

A female cheetah usually hunts only small animals, but male cheetahs hunting in a pack can tackle larger prey. Even when the cheetah has killed, it cannot be sure that it will be able to eat its prize. Hyenas or lions often rob a cheetah of its kill before the cheetah has time to eat.

When the cheetah has killed its prey, it is tired from making its high-speed dash and rests for a while to recover.

This cheetah is stalking its prey. It will drop to the ground in a crouch if the prey looks up.

But then it eats its kill very quickly, beginning at the stomach, and eating up to 30 pounds (14 kg) of meat. Four cheetahs together have been seen eating a whole impala in only 15 minutes!

The hunt is not always successful. A cheetah chasing an adult gazelle has only a slightly better than 50 percent chance of catching it. When a cheetah fails to make a kill, it has to rest for about 1½ hours to recover its strength before it can try again. When a cheetah still hasn't made a kill after three or four hunts, its exhaustion and hunger makes each new hunt more difficult.

Wildebeest are among the larger and stronger of the animals that a cheetah hunts. A successful catch means that there is plenty of food to eat.

Social Life

Cheetahs are not very sociable animals. Female cheetahs without cubs live alone, and so do 40 percent of male cheetahs. Other males form groups of two or three. They are often brothers. These groups usually defend a home range of about 15 square miles (40 km^2). Female home ranges are much larger. However, the ranges vary from area to area and from season to season. The cheetahs select high places in their home area and mark them by leaving piles of dung or by squirting urine on them. Visiting cheetahs may add their own dung or urine. These marked places seem to have a special social meaning. They alert visiting cheetahs that this area is already taken.

A male cheetah scent-marking its home area. For the moment, this is more important than chasing nearby prey.

The cheetah's home territories move to follow the prey, but while the cheetah family or group is in an area, it is possessive about that area. Cheetahs avoid going into territories where other groups are living. They are not usually hostile towards other cheetahs, but competition to be near females is fierce and males may chase other males out of their area. Male groups have a better chance of holding a territory than a single male. Half of all lone young male cheetahs die in battles when they try to invade territories held by male groups.

Cheetahs are active during times of the day when it is not too hot. They rest at night and during the middle of the day when the sun is strongest. They prefer to rest in a place where they cannot be seen easily.

To avoid a fight with a more powerful cheetah, a cheetah can indicate surrender by moaning and rolling on its back. Alternatively, the weaker cheetah may just sit on its haunches and look away, with a "pinched" expression.

In the heat of the middle of the day, cheetahs find a shady spot in which to sleep until the temperature drops.

Avoiding Danger

Cheetahs are timid animals and spend a lot of their time trying to avoid being seen. This is important because **predators** such as lions, hyenas, leopards, and humans are a big threat to them.

When resting, the cheetah lies down on its side in long grass or thick **vegetation**. Occasionally, it lifts its head to look for danger. Because its eyes are high up on its head, and it holds its ears low down against its head, it is difficult to see when hiding, even when its head is raised.

To avoid danger, a cheetah will sometimes simply freeze, hoping that its spotted coat will blend into the background as **camouflage** and make it invisible. Or the cheetah may

This cheetah cub resting in long grass is not easy for a predator to see, even with its head raised to look out for danger.

run away, sometimes making changes of direction to confuse the predator. Female cheetahs may deliberately draw predators away from hidden cubs.

Cheetahs have no real way of defending themselves, which is why they usually run away or hide when they are threatened. If the predator is an animal like a jackal, which is not too large, the cheetah may try to bluff its way out of trouble. It bares its teeth, hisses and snarls, and tries to frighten the attacker by arching its back and glaring at it, pretending it is going to attack. Then it makes sudden leaps forward and thumps the attacker with its forepaws. This form of mock attack can scare off a jackal, and two cheetahs were once seen chasing away eight hyenas!

A lion on the hunt is a very dangerous predator to a cheetah family. A lion can kill a whole litter of cubs.

Communication

Cheetahs make several sounds, which all have different meanings. When they are trying to scare a larger animal away, they moan, hiss, and growl. When members of the same cheetah family are far apart and want to make contact with each other, they make a short, high-pitched yipping sound. This can be heard up to 100 yards (90 m) away. They make the same sound when they are afraid.

Mother cheetahs have a range of sounds that lets them communicate with their cubs. A low-pitched sound tells the cubs to keep together and to keep still. A loud yelp or an "ee, ee" call tells the cubs to come and join her. A purring sound tells the cubs to follow her.

A successful hunt allows a cheetah to feed all her cubs. With a loud yelp she calls the young cheetahs to their dinner.

When cheetahs that know each other meet, they often let out a soft chirruping sound. This sound seems to show excitement. It is also heard when a cheetah has made a kill, or when males are sniffing around a female who is ready to mate. Young cheetahs at a kill make a whirring noise, which turns into a high-pitched squeal if they start fighting over the meat.

Like other cats, cheetahs purr. Young cheetahs are very playful animals and often purr as they play. Friendly cheetahs will sniff each other, lick each other's faces, and rub their cheeks together, purring at the same time.

Cheetahs in a friendly group often groom each other.

Bringing Up Young

Females that successfully raise their cubs may give birth to cubs every 20 months. Females that lose their cubs may reproduce after much shorter intervals. In East Africa, births usually take place between January and August. In Namibia and in South Africa most cheetahs give birth in November, December, and January.

The female cheetah has a period of 7 to 14 days when she can mate. During this time, her courtship behavior can seem violent. She will roll in front of a possible suitor, bound away, then return to him. She may also run her claws in front of his face, or lick and groom his chin. Male cheetahs also behave aggressively in their courtship. They

A female cheetah rests with her litter of four cubs.

may knock the female over and hit her, or even bite her. A female in heat (ready to mate) who enters the territory belonging to a group of male cheetahs can be kept in a "mating circle" surrounded by the males for several days while mating takes place.

A female's pregnancy lasts for 90 to 95 days. She finds a safe place under a bush for the birth. The female usually has a litter of one to four cubs, although there have been litters of eight. The newborn cubs, like other species, are blind, and they are clumsy when they try to move around. But they can spit violently when they are threatened.

For the first few weeks of life, the cubs suckle milk from their mother. Their eyes open when they are between four

Cheetah cubs suckle milk from their mother until they are three months old or older. This is all the food they need during most of this time.

and eleven days old, and when they are three weeks old their teeth begin to appear. By three weeks, the cubs can walk quite well. At eight weeks, they are able to follow their mother about.

The mother changes the site of the new family's home, sometimes as often as once a day. This is to keep the cubs safe from predators. The mother takes care when returning to the shelter to make sure that no predators are watching.

The cubs soon need to eat meat, so the mother must go hunting for them. This is a difficult time for her, because

These two cheetah cubs are resting, perhaps after playing. Cheetahs are very playful when young.

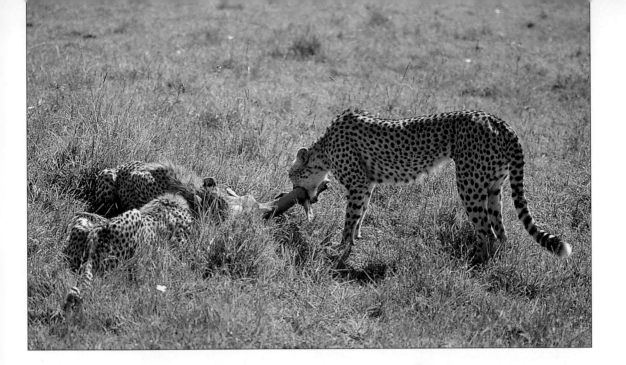

while she is hunting she cannot protect her young. After a successful kill, the mother calls her young to her, and the whole family joins in the meal. The mother is sometimes too exhausted to eat before she has rested, but this does not stop the cubs from starting on their food!

At three months old, the cubs need to eat meat at least once every three days. This puts a heavy burden on their mother. One mother, who was filmed looking after her two cubs in Tanzania, did not manage to feed her family for two days. On the first day, her hunt failed. On the second day, her kill was stolen from her by a hyena. Only on the third day, when she was becoming exhausted from hunger and the effort of the chase, did she manage to make a kill and call her cubs to eat.

Only one in 20 cheetah cubs survives to adulthood. The period when the young cubs are left unprotected by the mother because she has to hunt is one of the most

Here an impala has failed to outrun a cheetah with two large and hungry cubs to feed.

These six-week-old cubs are playing, but their games teach them the skills they will need as as adults. Tree-climbing is one.

dangerous times. Many cubs are eaten by predators. Sometimes cubs starve to death, perhaps because their mother cannot kill sufficient prey to feed them, or because she herself is killed by a predator. Sometimes she just abandons them.

Between the ages of three and six months, the cubs grow very rapidly. They play together, imitating the movements of hunting by chasing each other, batting each other with their forepaws, leaping into the air and spinning around. The cubs also climb trees and pretend to fight.

When the cubs are about eight months old, the mother starts to teach them to hunt properly. They practice stalking prey, and if the prey is small and young enough, the cubs may make a kill. When they are one year old, the young cheetahs are old enough to start hunting alone.

As the cubs become older they can follow their mother around and start to learn how to hunt.

Saving the Cheetah

Although the cheetah is a protected species, its **population** worldwide is still shrinking. Cheetahs were once common over much of Africa and Asia; now they live only in parts of Africa and Iran. Cheetah populations have become so small because their **habitats** and prey have been destroyed by humans. In the past, cheetahs were also killed for their fur, but this is now banned.

In South and East Africa, where most of the world's cheetahs now live, the animals are more likely to survive if they do not live in one of the game **reserves**. Inside the reserves the cheetahs are threatened by larger animals, such as lions, and have to compete with them for food.

Leopard and cheetah skins. It is now against the law to hunt either of these protected species for their fur.

The cheetahs that live on farmland are also at risk. Ranchers are allowed to shoot cheetahs if they think the animals are killing their cattle.

No one really knows how many cheetahs there are left in the world. In the 1950s, it was estimated that there were only about 28,000. By the early 1970s, their numbers had dropped to 14,000, and by 1993 there were around 10,000 in Africa and 50 in Iran. **Captive breeding** in zoos is more and more successful, but it is difficult to release the animals into the wild. In Namibia, Africa, some farmers have put donkeys with calving cattle since donkeys have been known to chase away cheetahs. It is hoped that more will be done in the future to protect this shy, wonderful animal.

"Sandy," an orphan cheetah kept in a game reserve in Tanzania, Africa. Cheetahs such as Sandy can now be successfully bred in captivity.

Useful Addresses

For more information about cheetahs and how you can help protect them, contact these organizations:

African Wildlife Foundation
1717 Massachusetts Avenue NW
Suite 602
Washington, D.C. 20036

Cheetah Conservation Fund
2162 Baldwin Road
Ojai, CA 93023

Kenya Wildlife Fund
P.O. Box 2445, Station B
Richmond Hill
Ontario L4E 1A5

The Wildlife Conservation Society
185th Street and Southern Blvd.
Bronx, NY 10460

World Wildlife Fund
1250 24th Street NW
Washington, D.C. 20037

World Wildlife Fund Canada
90 Eglinton Avenue East
Suite 504
Toronto
Ontario M4P 2Z7

Further Reading

Built for Speed: the Extraordinary, Enigmatic Cheetah Sharon Thompson
   (Minneapolis: Lerner Publications, 1998)
Cheetah Caroline Arnold (New York: Morrow Junior Books, 1989)
Cheetah! Taylor Morrison (New York: Henry Holt, 1989)
Endangered Wildlife of the World (New York: Marshall Cavendish
   Corporation, 1994)

Glossary

Adaptable: Able to change to suit different conditions.

Camouflage: Marking or coloring that helps an animal blend into its surroundings so that it is not easily seen.

Captive breeding: Encouraging captive cheetahs to produce cubs.

Carnivore: A species, such as cheetahs, lions, wolves, cats, that eats meat.

Family: A group of animal or plant species.

Habitat: The place where an animal lives. For example, a cheetah's habitat is semi-desert, grassland plains, and bushland.

Mammal: A kind of animal that is warm-blooded and has a backbone. Most are covered with fur or have hair. Female mammals produce milk to feed their young.

Mate: 1) When a male and female get together to produce young; 2) An animal's partner, with which it breeds.

Population: A number of animals that live in the same area and are able to breed together.

Predator: An animal that hunts other animals for food.

Prey: An animal that is hunted and eaten by another animal.

Range: The area of the world where an animal is found.

Reserve: Land that has been set aside where plants and animals can live without being harmed.

Species: A type of animal or plant. Animals of the same species look alike and can breed together.

Stalk: To approach prey quietly and carefully, hoping not to be seen.

Subspecies: Within a species, animals and plants can be divided into smaller groups that are slightly different from each other.

Ungulate: A mammal, such as deer and horses, that has hooves.

Vegetation: Plant life, such as grass, bushes, and trees.

Index